Karl Marx:

A WORLD WITHOUT JEWS

Books by Dagobert D. Runes

A
WORLD
WITHOUT
JEWS

By KARL MARX

Translated from the Original German

With an introduction by Dagobert D. Runes

PHILOSOPHICAL LIBRARY

New York

ISBN: 978-0-8065-2953-0

Printed in the United States of America

INTRODUCTION

It is with some reluctance that I have agreed to write these introductory lines to Karl Marx's embittered review of the Jewish problem. My reluctance is caused by the awareness that the Marxian type of anti-Semitism is still virulent among those furtive few who find in Jew hatred a compensative way of living out the envies of their drab existences.

On the other hand, our present era has been offered the repeated spectacle of the yellow badge of anti-Semitism attached to banners allegedly flying for Socialism.

Almost a generation ago, the National Socialist Party of Germany adorned its Staffel with that badge, and in our living days the red flag of the Soviet Union carries next to the hammer and sickle the hooked cross.

Was it just an ill wind of history that brought the evil odor of Jew hatred into these humanitarian camps of Socialist movements? Or are we faced here with a situation of direct cause and effect?

I should like to cite a few paragraphs from the booklet that lies before you. These lines which I am quoting are not from the pen of Adolf Hitler or Colonel Nasser, but verbatim translations from the German original of the Father of Socialism, Karl Marx:

"Money is the zealous one God of Israel, beside which no other God may stand. Money degrades all the gods of mankind and turns them into commodities. Money is the universal and self-constituted value set upon all things. It has therefore robbed the whole world, of both nature and man, of its original value. Money is the essence of man's life and work, which have become alienated from him: this alien monster rules him and he worships it.

"The God of the Jews has become secularized and is now a worldly God. The bill of exchange is the Jew's real God. His God is the illusory bill of exchange.

"What is the foundation of the Jew in our world? Practical necessity, private advantage.

"What is the object of the Jew's worship in this world? Usury. What is his worldly God? Money.

"Very well then: emancipation from usury and money, that is, from practical, real Judaism, would constitute the emancipation of our time."

* * *

Some readers may raise the question in their minds, what attitude are we to take toward this man who was himself a Jew? To those readers, I reply that in the middle of the nineteenth century anti-Semitism was mainly a religious and social, not a racial, issue, and among converts such as Karl Marx are to be found vitriolic enemies of Judaism. The convert as a tool in the hands of professional Jew baiters is to be found as early as the Middle Ages in the person of the Jew Pfefferkorn who assisted in attempts to put Jewish sacred literature to the torch. And little more than ten years ago in the Soviet Union, the Jew Ilya Ehrenburg led the attack against Jewish writers as being cosmopolitan, non-patriotic and Zionist. This he did at the grave of almost eight hundred Yiddish poets, writers, and novelists who had been executed at the behest of Stalin.

Karl Marx was not only born a Jew; he came from a rabbinical family. His father Heschel Marx accepted Christianity in 1816 in order to practice law in Prussian territory. Like many converts, Marx found it necessary all his life to justify the mass conversion of his family by attacks against his blood brothers.

Anti-Semitic expressions of his are to be found mainly in the present essay, in his *Class Struggles in France*, *In the Eighteenth Brumaire of Louis Bonaparte*, and in his *Letters to Engels*, censored by Bebel and Bernstein. Some of the editors of his writings attempted to modify the vindictiveness of Marx's aggression. Others, like Mehring, even intensified them.

* * *

I should like to quote at random a few more examples of Marxian Jew baiting:

"It is the circumvention of law that makes the religious Jew a religious Jew." (*Die Deutsche Ideologie*, MEGA V, 162)

"The Jews of Poland are the smeariest of all races." (*Neue Rheinische Zeitung*, April 29, 1849)

He called Ferdinand Lassalle, "Judel Itzig—Jewish Nigger." (*Der Jüdische Nigger*, MEKOR III, 82, July 30, 1862)

"Ramsgate is full of Jews and fleas." (MEKOR IV, 490, August 25, 1879)

* * *

The identification of Judaism with usury and exploitation of the masses, combined with an alleged secret master plan of the Jews with headquarters in Jerusalem to dominate the rest of the world, has been, and still is, the fundamental platform of political anti-Semitism. Copies of Hitler's *Mein Kampf* and Russia's *Protocols of Zion* have only recently been distributed by Khrushchev's close ally, Colonel Nasser. The late President Zapotocki of Communist Czechoslovakia declared at the time of the mass trials of Jews within the Soviet empire, in reply to protest from the free world, "We will not submit to the Jerusalem-New York axis."

Today in Marxist Russia no Jewish magazine or newspaper may be published, no Jewish cultural center may function, no Jewish rituals may be publicly observed. No Jew may hold major public office or be a member of the Soviet parliament, and even harboring any expression of Zionist character is dealt with as a capital offense.

We also note that in other sectors of the Soviet empire Marxian anti-Semitism is visible. Mao Tse-Tung, the undisputed leader of Red China, declared Israel to be "the Formosa of the Mediterranean" which should be swept into the sea. The Socialist Nehru of India, an ardent admirer of Colonel Nasser, does not permit the liberal and democratic State of Israel to open an embassy, or even a consulate, anywhere in India.

The German as well as the Russian forms of Socialism, be they national or international, have never freed themselves of the taint of a malevolent Jew hatred. And while among the peoples of the free world anti-Semitism has not been completely eradicated, in the West it is only the lunatic fringe that launches propaganda against the Hebrews, while in the Communist domain, the governments themselves spearhead the drive against the ancient people.

The Marxist tendency of identifying Judaism with Mammonism and usury is discernible throughout the Socialist movements of Germany, Austria and Russia.

It is therefore not surprising that Adolf Hitler was able to take over the Marxist unions of Germany almost unchecked. In spite of the brown and red differences, they found themselves to be brothers under the skin in forming a common front against an illusory conquestorial Zionism.

The so-called ideological purges of Stalin were little more than a cover-up for an anti-Semitic onslaught in the Soviet empire, which later engulfed Rumania, Poland, Hungary and Czechoslovakia.

As Khrushchev himself confessed, Stalin planned to relegate all the Jews of Russia to the marshlands of Biro-Bidjan in Siberia. On the other hand, the very same Khrushchev stated, paraphrasing Hitler, that Jews could not work in a co-operative society, and he publicly admitted having for that very reason reintroduced the Czarist *numerus clausus* in all schools of higher education in the Soviet Union. This, together with an official anti-Semitic policy combined with a Draconic suppression of all Jewish cultural activities, has succeeded in reducing the Jewish population of Soviet Russia to the status of a colonial people, confined to basically menial and subordinate tasks.

A further threat, through the classification of every act of religious or cultural Judaism as political Zionism, and therefore a capital criminal act, has driven the

Jewish population of Russia into a spiritual house-ghetto. Persons of the Jewish faith do not today dare to practice or observe even the most ancient religious rites in the face of the wanton terror displayed by the dominant Marxist government.

The cunning distinction made by the Soviet leaders and their fellow travelers between Zionism and Judaism is similar to the old Marxist differentiation between the Capitalist Jew and the Sabbath Jew, the Hitler abstraction of International Jew or Cosmopolitan Jew and Commonplace Jew. The people of Soviet Russia today rarely, if ever, are aware of these fine, ignoble shades, and develop in themselves under the relentless propaganda of the Kremlin an almost physical disdain for their Jewish neighbors, just as the people of Germany and Poland absorbed the malevolent Jew-hatred of the Marx-Hitler brand, in spite of the fine-mesh, allegedly protective screening in the uncanny segregation of International Zionism from Sabbath Judaism.

There is no Sabbath Judaism without Zionism. Every daily prayer of the observing Jew carries the undertone of return to Zion. The four great holidays of the Jewish faith are imbedded in Zionist law and Zionist home-coming. Judaism is as little possible without Zionism as Christianity without Christ. It is in this knowledge that Marxist masters of the Soviet empire attempt to prohibit all religious practice of the Jews, because of their being all of Zionistic character. The distinction between Judaism and Zionism is made by the Marxist elements purely to confound the uninitiated and make a pogrom appear like a political police action.

The official Soviet Socialist attitude toward Israel and the Jewish people in general was unmistakably stated in their State publication of 1958, entitled *The State of Israel—Its Position and Policies*, by K. Ivanov and Z. Sheinis.

From this State document we translate ". . . The Zionist movement represents a form of the nationalistic ideology of the rich Jewish bourgeoisie, intimately tied to imperialism and to colonial oppression of the people of Asia. Zionism has tied itself to American and other Western capitalism and, with Jewish terrorist tactics, attacked its Arab neighbors. The national liberation movement of the people of the Middle East, spearheaded by its native leaders (such as President Nasser, King Ibn Saud of Saudi Arabia and King Iman Ahmad of Yemen) is constantly threatened by naked Jewish aggression . . ."

"The clear duty of all Marxists and Communists in this situation is to help the Asian and African people crush the reactionary Jewish forces."

Such reads the widely-propagated platform of the Khrushchev-Mao Marxist axis. In fundamentals, it differs little from the Hitler-Stalin resolves of a generation ago, and it forebodes no less terror today than the previous anti-Jewish onslaught. Marxism may have failed in many of its postulates and prognostications, but its anti-Semitism lives on unabated.

It is indeed possible that these terrorist practices may succeed where the Roman *soldateska* of Titus and the pyres of Torquemada failed, namely, to bring to reality the sanguinary dream of Karl Marx—a world without Jews.   D.D.R.

FOREWORD

The booklet presented here is the first unexpurgated English language publication of papers written by Karl Marx originally published in Germany as a review of the writings of Dr. Bruno Bauer, a contemporary theologian and social philosopher, on "the Jewish question." [1]

It is interesting to note that most of Marx's anti-Semitic references, in his correspondence, his journalistic writings and his books, were entirely eliminated by his various editors. Their full text, however, is now being published by the decidedly anti-Jewish-oriented State Publishing House in Moscow.

The following main references were used:

Collected Works of Karl Marx and Friedrich Engels, 1841-1850, Vol. I, March 1841-March 1844, edited by Franz Mehring, Stuttgart, Dietz Nachf., 1902.

Marx-Engels Gesamtausgabe, MEGA, Moscow, 1927-1935; *Marx-Engels Gesamtausgabe,* Third Section, MEKOR, Berlin, 1929-1931.

The State of Israel—Its Position and Policies by K. Ivanov and Z. Sheinis, edited by I. Dinerstein, State Publishers of Political Literature, Moscow, 1958.

[1] *The Jewish Question,* Braunschweig, 1843. *The Capacity of Today's Jews and Christians to Become Free,* Zurich and Winterthur, Georg Herwegh. 1843.

I. THE JEWISH QUESTION

German Jews seek emancipation. What kind of emancipation? Civil and political emancipation.

Bruno Bauer answers them as follows: No one in Germany is politically emancipated. We non-Jews are unfree. How can we free you? You Jews are being egotists when you demand special emancipation as Jews. You should, rather, be working as Germans for the political emancipation of Germany and as men for the emancipation of mankind. You should learn to regard the peculiar form of your oppression not as an exception to, but as a confirmation of, the rule.

Or do Jews simply demand equality with Christian subjects of the state? In that case they recognize the Christian state as the legitimate one and recognize that it is a regime of universal subjection. Why do they object to their particular yoke while accepting the universal yoke? Why should Germans become interested in the liberation of Jews when Jews are not interested in the liberation of Germans?

The Christian state knows only privileges. In that state the Jew has the privilege of being a Jew. As a Jew, he has rights that Christians do not have. Why then does he want rights he does not have but which Christians do?

When the Jew demands emancipation from the Christian state, he asks that the Christian state give up its religious prejudice. Does he, the Jew, give up *his* religious prejudice? What right, therefore, has he to demand of others the abdication of their religion?

The Christian state cannot by its very nature emancipate the Jew; but, Bauer adds, the Jew cannot, by *his* very nature, be emancipated. As long as the state remains Christian and the Jew Jewish, the one is as incapable of granting emancipation as the other is of receiving it.

The Christian state can behave toward the Jew only in the manner of a Christian state, that is, in a privilege-conferring manner. It permits the separation of the Jew from its other subjects but makes him feel the pressure of the groups from which it has separated him, all the more acutely in that he represents religious opposition to the ruling religion. But the Jew, in turn, can behave toward the state only in a Jewish manner, that is, as a stranger. He opposes to real nationality his chimerical nationality, to real law his illusory laws; he feels that his separation from the rest of mankind is justified; he does not participate in the movement of history as a matter of principle; he waits for a future that has nothing in common with the general future of man; he regards himself as a member of the Jewish people and the Jewish people is for him the chosen people.

On what grounds, therefore, do you Jews demand emancipation? On the grounds of your religion? It is the deadly enemy of the state religion. As citizens of the state? There exist no true citizens in Germany. As human beings? You are no more human than those to whom you appeal.

-2-

After criticizing the existing positions and the solutions proposed to them, Bauer considers the Jewish question from a new angle. What is the nature, he asks, of the Jew who seeks emancipation and of the state which is to emancipate him? He answers with a criticism of the Jewish faith, analyzing the religious opposition between Judaism and Christianity, and elucidating the character of the Christian state. He does this with boldness, acuteness, spirit and thoroughness, in language that is precise, vigorous and meaningful.

How does Bauer solve the Jewish question? His formulation of the question itself contains his solution. An analysis of the Jewish question provides the answer to it. His analysis can be summarized as follows:

We must emancipate ourselves before we can emancipate others.

The stiffest form of opposition between Jew and Christian is religious. How is it to be resolved? By making it impossible. How can this be achieved? By abolishing religion. As soon as Jew and Christian recognize their respective religions as different stages in the evolution of the human spirit, as successive snakeskins shed by history—man being the snake that bore them all—they will no longer stand in a religious relationship to each other, but in a critical, scientific, human relationship. Science is their ground of unity, and contradictions in science are resolved by science itself.

The German Jew in particular is faced with a lack of political emancipation in a state that is avowedly Christian. But Bauer holds that the Jewish question has universal significance, independent of the specific German situation. It is, for him, a question of the relations between church and state and of the contradiction between religious ties and political freedom. Emancipation from religion is presented as a condition both to the Jew who is to be emancipated politically and to the state which is to emancipate him as well as itself.

"Very well," one says—and the Jew himself says it—"the Jew is to be emancipated not as Jew, not because he possesses such broad ethical principles; he is, rather, to fall in line with other citizens and become one of them *in spite of* being a Jew and wanting to remain one. That means he is and remains a Jew in spite of his being a citizen living in typical human circumstances: his limited character as a Jew always wins in the end, even over his human and political obligations. The prejudice remains, even though it is overtaken by general principles. But if it remains, then it takes over everything else. . . .

"The Jew can remain a Jew in political life only sophistically, only in appearance. If he wants to remain a Jew this appearance becomes reality and triumphs. This means that his life in a state is only an appearance and an exception to reality and rule."

Let us see how Bauer views the duty of the state.

"France," he says, "has recently offered us, with regard to the Jewish question—and with regard to all other political questions—the spectacle of a life which is free but which revokes its freedom by law, that is, it proclaims freedom a mere appearance and contradicts free law by deeds . . .

"Universal freedom is not yet law in France, nor is the Jewish question solved there, because the legal freedom which makes all citizens equal is limited in actual life, which is still ruled and divided by religious privilege. This lack of freedom in real life turns on the law and forces it to divide citizens, in themselves free, into oppressors and oppressed."

When will the Jewish question be solved in France?

"The Jew would cease being a Jew if he stopped letting his Law prevent him fulfilling his duties toward the state and his fellow citizens—for instance, if he went to the Chamber of Deputies on the Sabbath and took part in public debates. All religious privileges, including the monopoly of a privileged church, would have to be abolished, and if a man, or some men, or the overwhelming majority of men, still believed it necessary to fulfill religious duties, such fulfillment would be left a purely private matter. . . .

"Religion no longer exists when there is no privileged religion. Take from religion its exclusive power and it ceases to exist. . . . Just as M. Martin du Nord felt that the proposal not to mention Sunday in the law was a proposal to declare that Christianity no longer existed, it may be assumed with equal justice that a declaration that the Sabbath law is no longer binding on Jews would amount to a proclamation that Judaism had been dissolved."

Thus Bauer asks, on the one hand, that the Jew give up Judaism, and man generally give up religion, in order to achieve political emancipation. On the other hand, he holds that the political abolition of religion means the abolition of religion as such. A state which assumes religion is not yet a true, a real state. "The religious concept does, indeed, offer guarantees to the state. But to which state? To what kind of state?"

It is here that Bauer's one-sided presentation of the Jewish question becomes apparent.

It is by no means enough to investigate the question who is to emancipate and who emancipated. Still a third kind of question must be subjected to analysis: What kind of emancipation is at stake? What conditions are assumed by the kind of emancipation demanded? Only an analysis of political emancipation itself provides an ultimate analysis of the Jewish question and its inclusion in "the universal questions of our time."

Since Bauer does not raise the question to this level he falls into contradictions. He presents conditions which are not based on the true nature of political emancipation. He raises questions which are not pertinent to his problem and solves problems that leave his questions unanswered. Bauer says of the enemies of Jewish emancipation that "their mistake lay in assuming the Christian state to be the only true one and failing to subject it to the same criticism as the Jews." We hold that Bauer's error consists in subjecting only "the Christian state" to criticism, rather than the state as such, and in failing to investigate the relation of political emancipation to the larger emancipation of mankind, so that he presents conditions that can only be explained by an uncritical confusion between political emancipation and human emancipation in general. Bauer asks the Jews: "Have you, from your own point of view, the right to demand emancipation?" We, on the contrary, ask: "Has the champion of political emancipation the right to demand of the Jews the abolition of Judaism, and of mankind the abolition of religion?"

The Jewish question receives a different formulation depending on the country in which the Jew finds himself. In Germany, where there is no political state as such, the Jewish question is a purely theological one. The Jew finds himself in religious opposition to a state which believes that Christianity is its basis. This state is a theologian *ex professo*. Criticism here is twofold, of both Christian and Jewish theology. And so we are still operating, however critically, in the sphere of theology.

In France, a constitutional state, the Jewish question is a constitutional one, a question of the incompleteness of political emancipation. Since France maintains the appearance of a state religion, even though by the empty and self-contradictory formula of "the religion of the majority," the relation of the Jew to the state still maintains the appearance of a religious, a theological opposition.

It is only in the free states of North America—or at least in some of them—that the Jewish question loses its theological character and becomes a truly secular one. Only where the political state exists in completely realized form can the relation of the Jew, and of the religious man generally, to the state appear in all its purity and peculiarity. Analysis of this relationship ceases to be theological as soon as the state ceases to stand in a theological relation to religion and replaces that relationship with a political one. Criticism then becomes a criticism of the political state.

It is at this point, where the question ceases to be theological, that Bauer's critique ceases to be critical: "*Il n'existe aux Etats-Unis ni religion d'état, ni religion déclarée celle de la majorité, ni prééminence d'un culte sur un autre. L'état est étranger à tous les cultes.*" ("There exists in the United States no state religion nor any religion proclaimed to be that of the majority, nor pre-eminence of one religion over another. The state is foreign to all religions.") (*Marie ou l'esclavage aux Etats-Unis,* by G. de Beaumont, Paris, 1835.) Indeed, there are some American states where "*la constitution n'impose pas les croyances religieuses e la pratique d'un culte comme condition des privilèges politiques*" ("the constitution does not impose religious belief and the practice of a religion as the condition of political rights"). All the same, "*on ne croit pas aux Etats-Unis qu'un homme sans religion puisse être un honnête homme*" ("in the United States it is not believed that a man without religion can be a gentleman"). Nonetheless, America is peculiarly the land of religiosity, as Beaumont, Tocqueville and the Englishman Hamilton unanimously agree.

But the American states serve only as an example. The question is: What is the relation of full political emancipation to religion? If we find even in the land of full political emancipation that religion not only exists, but blossoms fresh and strong, we have proof that the existence of religion is not opposed to the full development of the state. But since the existence of religion is the existence of a defect, the source of this defect can be sought only in the nature of the state. We hold that religion is no longer the operating cause but the result of human limitation. We therefore derive the religious small-mindedness of free citizens from their general small-mindedness. We do not maintain that they must abolish their religious limitations in order to abolish their human limitations. We do not turn secular human problems into religious ones; we turn religious questions into secular ones. History has too long been dissolved into superstitions: we now dissolve superstitions into history. The question of the relationship of political emancipation to religion becomes for us a question of the relationship of political emancipation to human emancipation. We criticize the religious weakness of the political state by criticizing, rather, its defective worldly constitution. We resolve the contradiction between the state and a particular religion, such as Judaism, into a contradiction between the state and certain secular elements, religion in general and the state's own assumptions.

The political emancipation of the Jew, the Christian or the religious man in general is a question of the emancipation of the state from Judaism, Christianity and religion in general. The state emancipates itself from religion, both as to form and content, by emancipating itself from any state religion—that is, by professing no religion except its own statehood. Political emancipation from religion is not emancipation from religion carried out without opposition because political emancipation is not human emancipation carried out without opposition.

The limit of political emancipation lies in the fact that the state can free itself from a limitation without its citizens becoming free from it, and that the state can be a free state without the man in it being a free man. Bauer himself admits this tacitly in setting the following condition of political emancipation: "All religious privilege, including the monopoly of a privileged church, would be abolished, and should some or many or even the overwhelming majority feel bound to fulfill religious obligations, such fulfillment would be their private affair." The state, therefore, can still emancipate itself from religion if its overwhelming majority is religious. And the overwhelming majority does not cease being religious by being religious only in private.

But the attitude of the state, and particularly of a free state, toward religion is only the religious attitude of the men who form the state. It follows from this that man frees himself from political limitations, through the intermediary of the state, by raising himself above this limitation, in an abstract, limited and partial manner. It also follows that when man frees himself politically, he necessarily frees himself indirectly, through an intermediary. It follows, finally, that when a man proclaims the state atheistic—he is still tied to religion because he proclaims himself only indirectly, through an intermediary. The state is the intermediary between man and his freedom. As Christ is the intermediary whom the Christian burdens with his divinity and all his religious ties, so the state is the intermediary whom man burdens with his entire non-divinity and his complete absence of ties.

The political triumph of man over religion shares all the advantages and disadvantages of political triumph generally. Thus, for example, the state annuls private property: man proclaims politically that private property is abolished as soon as he abolishes the property qualifications for the vote, as has been done in several American states. Politically speaking, Hamilton judges this fact quite correctly: "The great mass has won a victory over the owners of property and wealth." Is not private property as an idea abolished when the non-owner becomes legislator for the owner? The property qualification for the vote is the ultimate political form of the recognition of private property.

But political annulment of private property does not abolish the existence of private property; on the contrary, it necessarily assumes that existence. The state in its own way abolishes differences of birth, status, education and occupation when it proclaims that these differences are nonpolitical; when it makes every member of the people without regard to such differences an equal participant in popular sovereignty; when it judges all the elements making up the actual life of the people from the point of view of the state itself. Nonetheless the state permits private property, education and occupation to continue in themselves, that is, as private property, education and occupation, and to make their particular natures felt. Far from abolishing these activities, the state exists only through assuming their existence. It recognizes itself as a political organism and makes its over-all character felt only in opposition to these, its particular elements. And so Hegel correctly judges the relation of the political state to religion: "If the state is to come into being as a self-conscious, ethical and spiritual reality, it must be differentiated from the forms of authority and belief. But such a differentiation occurs only when the church itself is separated from it: the state can define the universal nature of its law, the principle of its form, and so bring itself into existence, only by opposing particular churches." (*Philosophy of Law*)

The perfect political state by its nature defines the life of man as of a particular kind, in opposition to his material life. In bourgeois society all the assumptions of this self-centered material life remain outside the sphere of the state, but they remain the characteristics of bourgeois society. Where the state has achieved true form, man leads a double life, not only in his thoughts and consciousness but in reality as well. It is both a heavenly and an earthly life—life in a political community, where he feels himself a member of the community, and life in bourgeois society, where he is active as a private individual, uses other men as means to an end and reduces himself to the same role of plaything of powers outside himself. Spiritually speaking, the state is to bourgeois society as heaven is to earth. It opposes it just as religion opposes and overcomes the secular world, by creating it, recognizing it, and letting itself be ruled by it. In bourgeois society man is a secular being. There, where he counts as an individual to himself and to others, he is an untrue phenomenon. In the state, however, where man counts merely as one of his kind, he is an imaginary link in an imagined chain of sovereignty, robbed of his individual life and endowed with an unreal generality.

The conflict in which man as believer in a particular religion finds himself, with his own citizenship and with other members of the community, is reduced to the secular split between the political state and bourgeois society. For the bourgeois man, "life in the state is only an appearance or a momentary exception to essence and rule." Indeed, the bourgeois, like the Jew, remains only sophistically in the state, just as the French *citoyen* remains a bourgeois or Jew only sophistically. But this sophistry is not personal; it is the sophistry of the state itself. The difference between the religious man and the citizen is the difference between the merchant and the citizen, the landowner and the citizen, the living individual and the citizen. The contradiction between the religious man and the political man is the same as that between the bourgeois and the *citoyen,* in which the member of bourgeois society, wearing his political lion's skin, finds himself.

Bauer permits this worldly conflict, to which the Jewish question is ultimately reduced, to continue by polemicizing against its religious expression. The conflict springs from the relation of the political state to its assumptions, whether they concern material elements, such as private property, etc., or spiritual ones, such as education, religion, the opposition between general and particular interests, etc. Bauer writes: "It is precisely its foundation, the need that establishes bourgeois society and makes it necessary, that maintains in it an element of insecurity and brings about this continuously changing mixture of wealth and poverty, of prosperity and adversity, indeed the very change itself."

Consider his whole chapter, "The Bourgeois Society," based on Hegel's philosophy of law. Bourgeois society in opposition to the political state is considered necessary because the political state is recognized as necessary.

Political emancipation is indeed a great goal. It is not the ultimate form of human emancipation, but it is the ultimate form possible within the present world order. And let it be understood that we mean real, practical emancipation.

Man emancipates himself from religion politically by relegating it from public to private law. It is no longer the spirit of the state, where man, in community with other men, behaves as a member of his kind, observing special forms in a special sphere. It has become the spirit of bourgeois society, of the sphere of egotism, of the *bellum omnium contra omnes*. It is no longer the essence of community but the essence of differentiation. It has become an expression of the differentiation of man from his communal nature, from himself and from other men—which was its original function. It is now only the abstract confession of a particular peculiarity, of a personal whim. The infinite splits of religion in the United States give it even the external appearance of a purely individual affair. It has been exiled from the sphere of the community as such and has been thrust among a crowd of private interests of which it is but one. But let there be no mistake about the limit of political emancipation. The splitting of man into private and public man, the dislocation of religion from the state in bourgeois society, is not a stage in political emancipation but its completion. It no more abolishes the true religiosity of man than it intends to abolish it.

The division of man into Jew and citizen, Protestant and citizen, religious man and citizen is not a lie against citizenship or a way to circumvent political emancipation: it is political emancipation itself, the political way of emancipation from religion. However, in a period in which the political state is brought forth violently from the womb of bourgeois society, when the liberation of man is sought in the form of political liberation, the state can—and indeed must—go so far as to abolish religion. But it must do so only in the way that it abolishes private property—by placing a maximum limit on it, by confiscation, by progressive taxation—or as it abolishes life itself—by the guillotine. In moments of especially acute self-consciousness, political life tends to smother its own presuppositions, that is, bourgeois society and its elements, and to constitute itself as the real and uncontradicted life of man as a member of the race. But it can do this only in violent contradiction to its own condition of existence, by proclaiming the revolution permanent. Otherwise, the political drama is bound to end with the restoration of religion, private property and all the elements of bourgeois society, as war is bound to end with peace.

The perfect Christian state is not the so-called Christian state which acknowledges Christianity as its official religion and excludes all others, but rather the atheistic state, the democratic state, which banishes religion to the level of other elements in bourgeois society. The state that remains theological, that continues to make an official profession of Christianity, has not yet succeeded in achieving the human basis of which Christianity is but an overwrought, worldly expression. The so-called Christian state is simply a nonstate, for it is not the Christian religion that expresses itself in human creations, but merely the human foundation of that religion.

The so-called Christian state is a Christian denial of the state, not in any way the political fulfillment of Christianity. The state that continues to profess Christianity as a religion does not yet profess it in political form because it still behaves religiously toward religion. This means that it is not a genuine fulfillment of the human basis of religion, because it is still the product of unreality, of the imaginary shape of the human nucleus. The so-called Christian state is the imperfect state, and it treats Christianity as a supplementation and sanctification of its imperfection. It treats religion as a means to an end and becomes thereby hypocritical. There is a great difference between a perfect state that counts religion as one of its assumptions because of a lack in the nature of the state, and an imperfect state which proclaims religion to be its very foundation because of a lack in its own make-up. In the latter case religion becomes imperfect politics; in the former the inability of religion to offer a perfect policy is immediately apparent. The so-called Christian state needs the Christian religion to complete itself as a state. The democratic state, the true state, requires no religion in order to be politically complete. It can indeed forego all religion because it achieves the human basis of religion in a worldly way. The so-called Christian state, on the other hand, behaves religiously toward politics and politically toward religion. Where it reduces the forms of politics to appearances, it likewise reduces religion to an appearance.

In order to express this contradiction clearly we need to examine Bauer's concept of the Christian state, a concept developed from that of the Christian-Germanic state. He writes:

"To prove the nonexistence or the impossibility of a Christian state it has recently been argued that there are certain passages in the Gospels which the state not only does not obey, but which it could not obey without dissolving itself. . . . But the matter cannot be dismissed so easily. What do these Biblical passages demand? Self-denial in favor of the Supernatural, submission to the authority of Revelation, a turning away from the state, the abolition of secular concerns. But this is all demanded and achieved by a Christian state. The state has made the spirit of the Gospels its own and if it does not render it in the exact words of the Gospels, that is because it expresses that spirit in its own forms. These forms follow from the nature of the state in this world, but they are reduced to an appearance by the religious rebirth they must undergo. It is the withdrawal from the state that uses the forms of the state to achieve itself."

Bauer goes on to describe how the people of a Christian state are a nonpeople who no longer have a will of their own but lead their existence through their ruler, to whom they are subject but who is by his very nature foreign to them, since he was given them by God without their being consulted in any way. Further, that the laws of such a people are not their own work but revelations handed down to them; that the ruler has to have privileged intermediaries between himself and the people; that the masses themselves divide into separate groups, accidentally determined and divided by special passions and prejudices, but permitted as a privilege to remain separate from each other; etc.; etc.

Bauer goes so far as to say: "If politics is to be nothing as religion, it cannot be politics, any more than the cleaning of cooking pots can be considered an economic matter if it is to be a religious matter." But in the Christian-Germanic state religion *is* an "economic matter," just as all "economic matter" is religion. In this state the religion of government is the government of religion.

The distinction between "the letter of the Gospel" and "the spirit of the Gospel" is an irreligious act. The state that lets the Gospel speak in political terms or, for that matter, in any other terms than those of the Holy Ghost, commits an act of sacrilege, if not in the eyes of men then in its own religious eyes. The state that regards Christianity as its highest expression and the Bible as its Charter must be made to come to terms with the words of Holy Writ, for the Gospel is holy in its every word. This state, along with the human law on which it is based, is placed in a painful contradiction that cannot be resolved by mere religious conviction, when it is made to face those pages of the Gospel which "it not only does not fulfill but which it could not fulfill without dissolving itself completely as a state." And why does it refuse to dissolve itself completely? It cannot answer this question, either to itself or to others. The official Christian state carries on its conscience an obligation whose carrying out is unachievable. The state can affirm its own existence only by lying to itself, and must therefore be a dubious, unreliable, problematical thing even to itself.

The critics are therefore fully justified in forcing such a state, which professes to stand on the Bible, into questioning its convictions, to discover whether they are real or figments of the imagination, and so that its infamous worldly purposes may be brought into plain conflict with its pious religious convictions, which declare religion to contain the meaning of life. Such a state might free itself from its internal conflicts by becoming the policeman of the Catholic Church. In relation to this Church, which proclaims worldly power its servant, the state is impotent, as is all worldly power which claims to be under the rule of the religious spirit.

What counts in the so-called Christian state is alienation, not man. The only man who does count, the king, is a creature who is designated different from other men, a divinely appointed creature directly related to Heaven and to God. The conditions that obtain here are still the conditions of faith. The religious spirit is therefore not yet secularized.

But the religious spirit *cannot* become secularized for it is nothing but the nonsecular form of the human spirit at a certain stage of its development. The religious spirit can realize itself only insofar as that stage of development of which it is the expression assumes a secular form. This is what happens in the democratic state. It is not Christianity but the human foundation of Christianity which is the foundation of this state. Religion remains the ideal, unworldly conviction of its members because it is the ideal expression of that particular stage of human development.

The members of the political state become religious by means of a dichotomy between their individual lives and the lives of the species, between the life of bourgeois society and its political life. They are religious insofar as man is related to life in the state, which is contrary to his real individuality, and insofar as their religion represents the spirit of bourgeois society and is an expression of the separation of man from man. Political democracy is Christian inasmuch as in it man —not just any man but every man— counts as of sovereign and ultimate worth. But this is man in his uncivilized and unsocial aspect, in his accidental existence, corrupted by the entire organization of our society, lost and alienated from himself, yielding to the rule of inhuman conditions and forces—in a word, man not yet a true member of his species. The dream creature of

-20-

imagination, the postulate of Christianity, the sovereign man—different from real man—is in democracy a sensual reality, a presence and a worldly symbol.

Religious and theological conviction counts in a democracy all the more for being apparently without political importance or earthly purpose, an affair of spirits in flight from the world, the expression of a limitation on reason, a product of whim and fancy, a truly other-worldly existence. Christianity here achieves its practical force as a universal religion by appropriating the most varied world views, while demanding of others not Christianity necessarily, but simply religion, any religion (see Beaumont, quoted above). Religious conviction glories in the wealth of contradictions and multiplicity of viewpoints in religion.

We have shown that political emancipation from religions permits religion to continue, though not privileged religion. The contradiction with his civil duties in which the adherent of any particular religion finds himself is merely one aspect of the general secular contradiction between the political state and bourgeois society. The perfect Christian state professes itself a state which ignores the religion of its citizens. The emancipation of the state from religion is not the emancipation of man from religion.

We do not, therefore, say to the Jews as Bauer does: "You cannot be politically emancipated unless you emancipate yourselves from Judaism." We say, rather, to them: Since you can become politically emancipated without abandoning Judaism completely, political emancipation will not bring you human emancipation. If you want to emancipate yourselves politically without emancipating yourselves humanly, the contradiction lies not merely in you; it lies also in the nature of political emancipation. If you are bound by this, then you share the general fetters. Just as the state dabbles in religion when it behaves toward the Jews in a Christian fashion, so the Jew dabbles in politics whenever he demands political rights.

But if a man can become politically emancipated and win civil rights even though he is a Jew, can he then also claim and win so-called human rights? Bauer denies this: "The question is whether the Jew as such—that is, the Jew who realizes that he is forced by his true nature to live in eternal separation from others—is able to receive general human rights and grant them to others. . . .

"The Christian world discovered the idea of human rights only in the last century. They are not inborn in man; they are, rather, won only after a struggle against the historical traditions in which man has hitherto been educated. Human rights are therefore not a gift from nature or a dowry from history, but the price of a struggle against the accident of birth and the privileges that history has passed on from generation to generation. They are the results of culture, and only he can possess them who has acquired them and won the right to them. . . .

"Has the Jew really earned this right? As long as he remains a Jew, the limited nature of his Jewishness triumphs over the human nature that would link him with other men, and separates him from non-Jews. By this separation he proclaims the special nature that makes him a Jew to be his true and highest nature, to which all human nature must yield. . . .

"In the same way, the Christian as Christian cannot grant human rights."

According to Bauer, man must sacrifice "the privilege of faith to be able to receive universal human rights." Let us consider for a moment these so-called human rights in their authentic expression, the expression they were given by their discoverers, the Americans and the French. These human rights are partly political rights, rights that can be exercised only in community with others. Participation in the community, the political community or state, provides their content. They fall under the category of political freedom, of civil rights, which, as we have seen, by no means presupposes the abolition of religion. That leaves for consideration those other human rights, the *droits de l'homme* (rights of man) as distinguished from the *droits du citoyen* (rights of the citizen).

Among these is freedom of conscience, the right to practice the religion of one's choice. The privilege of belief is implicitly recognized either as a human right or as a consequence of human rights (freedom).

"Nul ne doit être inquiété pour ses opinions même religieuses" ("No one must be disturbed on account of his beliefs, including religious ones"). (*Déclaration des droits de l'homme et du citoyen*, 1791, Article 10.) Article 1 of the Constitution of 1791 guarantees as a human right *"la liberté à tout homme d'exercer le culte*

religieux auquel il est attaché" ("every man's freedom to practice the religious worship to which he is attached").

The *Déclaration des droits* of 1793 includes among human rights, in Article 7: *"le libre exercice des cultes"* ("freedom of worship"). With regard to the right to publish one's views and opinions it even goes so far as to say:*"La nécessité d'énoncer ces droits suppose ou la présence ou le souvenir récent du despotisme"* ("The very need to proclaim these rights presupposes the presence or the recent memory of despotism").

The Constitution of Pennsylvania, Article 3, Paragraph 9, reads: "All men have received from nature the imprescriptible right to worship the Almighty according to the inspiration of their conscience and no one may be legally constrained to obey, institute or support against his will any worship or religious ministry. No human authority can, in any case, intervene in questions of conscience and control the powers of the soul."

The Constitution of New Hampshire, Articles 5 and 6, reads: "Among the natural rights some are inalienable by their nature because nothing can be their equivalent. Of such are the rights of conscience."

Incompatibility between religion and human rights is so far removed from the concept of human rights that the right to be religious, the right to be religious in a certain way, and the right to practice the worship of a given religion, are expressly enumerated among human rights. The privilege of belief is a universal human right.

The *droits de l'homme*, the rights of man as such, are distinguished from the *droits du citoyen*, the rights of the citizen. Who is this *"homme"* who is distinguished from the *citoyen?* None other than the member of bourgeois society. Why does the member of bourgeois society in this view become "man," plain man? Why are his rights called human rights? How can we explain this fact? By the relation between the state and bourgeois society, by the nature of political emancipation. Above all, we note that the *droits de l'homme* as distinguished from the *droits du citoyen* are none other than the rights of a member of bourgeois society, that is, of egotistical man, of man separated from the community. The most radical constitution, that of 1793, speaks for itself:

"Ces droits (les droits naturels et imprescriptibles) sont: l'égalité, la liberté, la sûreté, la propriété" ("These rights [natural and imprescriptible] are: equality, liberty, security and property"). (Article 2.)

What is *"liberté"?* Article 6 says: *"La liberté est le pouvoir qui appartient à tout homme de faire tout ce qui ne nuit pas aux droits d'autrui"* ("Liberty is the power belonging to each man to do anything that does not infringe the rights of others"), or as stated in the Declaration of Human Rights of 1791: *"La liberté consiste à pouvoir faire tout ce qui ne nuit pas à d'autrui"* ("Liberty consists in being able to do anything that does not harm others").

Liberty is thus the right to do anything that does not harm others. The limit within which each can move without harming others is determined by the law, just as the boundary between two fields is determined by a fence. It is the liberty of man conceived as an isolated man referring only to itself.

Why, then, is the Jew, according to Bauer, incapable of receiving human rights? "As long as he remains a Jew, the limited nature of his Jewishness wins out over the human nature that would link him as a man to other men, and separates him from non-Jews." But the human right of liberty is not based on the link between man and man, but rather on the separation of man from man. It is the right to this separation, the right to the individual limited to himself.

A practical example of the human right to liberty is the right of private property. What is that precisely?

"Le droit de propriété est celui qui appartient à tout citoyen de jouir et de disposer à son gré de ses biens, de ses revenus, du fruit de son travail et de son industrie" ("The right of property is the right belonging to each citizen of enjoying and disposing at will of his goods, his income, the fruits of his labor and industry"). (Article 16 of the Constitution of 1793.)

The human right of private property is thus the right to enjoy and dispose of one's wealth at will, without reference to others and independently of society; it is the right of private use. It is this freedom, and its practical applications, which forms the foundation of bourgeois society. It causes each man to find in his fellows not the realization of his freedom, but its limitation. It proclaims, above all, the human right *"de jouir et de disposer à son gré de ses biens, de ses revenus, du fruit de son traval et de son industrie."*

There remain those other human rights, *"égalité"* and *"sûreté."*

"Egalité" is used here in its nonpolitical sense; it is nothing but the equality of the *"liberté"* described above, that is, that every man is viewed equally as a monad sufficient unto himself. The Constitution of 1795 determined appropriately the importance and force of this equality: *"L'égalité consiste en ce que la loi est la même pour tous, soit qu'elle protège, soit qu'elle punisse"* ("Equality means that the law is the same for all, whether it protects or punishes"). (Article 5.)

And *"sûreté"*? *"La sûreté consiste dans la protection accordée à chacun de ses membres pour la conservation de sa personne, de ses droits et de ses propriétés"* ("Security consists of the protection offered by society to each of its members with regard to the preservation of their persons, their rights and their property"). (Article 8.)

Security is the highest social concept of bourgeois society, the police concept that the entire society exists only to assure each of its members the preservation of his person, his rights and his property. Hegel refers to this when he calls bourgeois society "the state of necessity and reason" (*Noth- und Verstandesstaat*).

Bourgeois society does not raise itself above its egotism through this concept of security. Security is, rather, an insurance of its egotism.

None of the so-called human rights, therefore, goes beyond the egotistical man, the man who, in bourgeois society, is separated from the community and withdrawn into himself, his private interest and his private will. Man is not conceived here as a member of his species; rather, the life of the species, that is, society, is conceived as a framework imposed upon individuals, a limitation of their original independence. The only bonds that hold them together are natural necessity, private interests, the conservation of property and their egotistical desires.

It is rather curious that a people just beginning to free itself, to break down the barriers between its individual members and form a political community, should solemnly proclaim the granting of rights to egotistical man, separated from his fellow men and from his community (Declaration of 1791). This people goes on to repeat this proclamation at a time when only the most heroic sacrifices can save its nation, when the sacrifice of all bourgeois interests has become the order of the day and egotism is punished as a crime (Declaration of 1793). All this becomes even more curious when we consider that citizenship in the political community was reduced by the political emancipators to the role of a mere means for the preservation of these so-called human rights. The *citoyen* is proclaimed servant of the egotistical *homme*; the sphere in which man acts as a member of his community is placed under the sphere in which he acts as a partial being. Finally, it is not even man as *citoyen,* but man as *bourgeois,* who is proclaimed the real, the true man.

"Le but de toute association politique est la conservation des droits naturels et imprescriptible de l'homme" ("The aim of all political association is the preservation

-28-

of the natural and imprescriptible rights of man"). (Declaration of 1791, Article 2.) *"Le gouvernement est institué pour garantir à l'homme la jouissance de ses droits naturels et imprescriptibles"* ("Government is instituted to guarantee man the enjoyment of his natural and imprescriptible rights"). (Declaration of 1793, Article 1.) So even in moments of youthful enthusiasm, fired by the urgency of circumstances, political life is proclaimed a mere means, the end of which is bourgeois society. True, the practice of the Revolution was a flagrant violation of its theory. While security was proclaimed a human right, the secrecy of correspondence was openly and daily violated. While the Constitution of 1793 guaranteed, in Article 122, *"la liberté indefinie de la presse"* ("unabridged freedom of the press") as a consequence of the right of individual freedom, in reality freedom of the press was completely abolished, for *"la liberté de la presse ne doit pas être permise lorsqu'elle compromet la liberté publique"* ("freedom of the press must not be permitted when it compromises public liberty") (Robespierre). This means simply that the human right of freedom ceases to be a right as soon as it conflicts with political realities, though the theory states that political life is a mere guarantee of human rights, the rights of individual man, and that it must be abolished as soon as it conflicts with those rights. But the practice is only the exception and the theory is the rule. If one chooses to regard revolutionary practice as the correct statement of the relationship, there still remains the mystery of why the relationship was turned on its head by the political emancipators so that ends appeared as means and vice versa.

The mystery is easily cleared up.

Political emancipation also meant the dissolution of the old society, upon which the state and the government power were founded. What was the character of that old society? One word defines it: feudalism. Old bourgeois society had a political character only indirectly, that is, such elements of bourgeois life as property, family, and kind and manner of work were raised to the level of political life through seignorial rights, estates or corporations. Only in these forms did they affect the relation of the individual to the state, that is, his political relation, his separation and exclusion from the other elements of society. For the feudal organization of national life did not raise work or property to the role of social elements; rather, it separated them from the state as a whole and constituted them as special societies within the total society. The functions and living conditions of bourgeois society were still political, if only in the feudal sense, that is, they separated the individual from the state as a whole; they converted his special relation to the state into a general relation to national life, and his special bourgeois activity and position into a general activity and position. The consequence of this social organization was that the state, in all its activities, that is, the governing power in general, was the special concern of the ruler and his servants, divorced from the people.

The revolution which dethroned this power and

turned the affairs of the state into the affairs of the people, and the political state into the affair of all—that is, the true state—inevitably destroyed all the estates, corporations, guilds and privileges which were so many varying expressions of the separation of the people from its community. The political revolution thus abolished the political character of bourgeois society. It broke up bourgeois society into its simple constituents: on the one hand the individuals, and on the other the material and spiritual elements that composed the bourgeois life of these individuals. It set loose the political spirit that had been scattered and concealed in the various cul-de-sacs of feudal society. It gathered up its parts, freed it from bourgeois life and turned it to the service of the community, the universal concern of the people, for an ideal independence from the elements of bourgeois life. Special activities and statuses sank to the level of the individual importance. They no longer comprised the relation of the individual to the state as a whole. Public concern became the general concern of each individual and political function became a universal function.

But the achievement of idealism in the state meant at the same time the achievement of bourgeois materialism. The shaking off of the yoke became the shaking off of the bonds that had fettered the egotistical spirit of bourgeois society. Political emancipation meant the emancipation of bourgeois society from politics, from even the appearance of having a content.

Feudal society was resolved into its basis, into man—but into man as he really was, egotistical man.

This man, the member of bourgeois society, is now the basis, the presupposition, of the political state. He is recognized as such in the various declarations of human rights.

The recognition of the freedom of egotistical man, however, is the recognition of the unrestrained movement of spiritual and material elements that form its content.

Man, therefore, was not freed from his religion but received religious freedom. He was not freed from property but received freedom of property. He was not freed from professional egotism but received freedom to practice it professionally.

The constitution of the political state is the dissolution of bourgeois society into separate individuals, whose relationship is based on rights, whereas that of the men in estates and guilds was based on privilege. But man, as a member of bourgeois society, as unpolitical man, necessarily appears to be "natural man." Thus the *droits de l'homme* appear to be *droits naturels,* for self-conscious activity concentrates on the political act. Egotistical man is the passive product of a dissolved society, the object of direct certainty and therefore a natural object. Political revolution resolves bourgeois life into its constituent parts without submitting these parts to a revolutionary examination. It treats bourgeois society —the world of needs, works, private interests and rights—as the foundation of its existence, as an assumption that needs no further justification, as its natural basis. Finally, man as a member of bourgeois society counts himself truly man, *homme* as distinguished from *citoyen,* because he is man in his sensual, individual and immediate existence while political man is abstract and artificial man, man as an allegorical and moral being. Real man is recognized in the shape of the egotistical *homme,* true man in the shape of the abstract *citoyen.*

"Celui qui ose entreprendre d'instituer un peuple doit se sentir en état de changer, pour ainsi dire la nature humaine, de transformer chaque individu, qui par lui-même est un tout parfait et solitaire en partie d'un plus grand tout, dont cet individu reçoive, en quelque sorte sa vie et son être, de substituer une existence partielle et morale à l'existence physique et indépendante. Il faut qu'il ôte à l'homme ses forces propres pour lui en donner qui lui soient étrangères et dont il ne puisse faire usage sans le secours d'autrui."

("He who dares the undertaking of starting a people must feel himself capable, so to speak, of changing human nature, of transforming each individual, who is in himself a perfect and separate unit, into part of a larger whole from which he will in some way receive his life and existence, and of substituting a partial and moral existence for an independent and physical one. He must take away from man his own powers and give him in return powers which are alien to him and which he cannot use without the help of others.") (*Social Contract, Book I,* London, 1757.)

All emancipation is a reduction of the human world, of human relations, to man himself.

Political emancipation is the reduction of man, on the one hand to the status of membership in bourgeois society, to the egotistical and independent individual, and on the other to the status of citizen, to the moral person.

Human emancipation is achieved only when the individual gives up being an abstract citizen and becomes a member of his species as individual man in his daily life and work and situation, when he recognizes and organizes his "*forces propres,*" his own strength, as part of the forces of society, which are then no longer separated from him as a political power.

II. THE CAPACITY OF TODAY'S JEWS AND CHRISTIANS TO BECOME FREE

Under this title Bauer deals with the relationship between the Christian and the Jewish religions and the relationship of religion to "the capacity to become free."

His conclusion is this: "The Christian has only one stage to go in order to abolish religion altogether (that is, to become free). . . .The Jew, on the other hand, has to break not only with his own Jewish nature but also with the perfectionist trend of his religion, a trend to which he has remained essentially alien."

Bauer thus turns the question of Jewish emancipation into a purely religious one. The old theological argument as to who has the better prospect of salvation, Christian or Jew, is repeated in a new form: Which of the two is more capable of emancipation? The question is no longer: Is it Judaism or Christianity which makes one free? It is, on the contrary: Is it the negation of Judaism or of Christianity which makes one freer?

"If the Jews want to be free they should embrace Christianity, but a dissolved Christianity, dissolved religion in general, that is, enlightenment, the critical spirit and its consequence, a free humanity."

And so there is still left a profession of faith for the Jews, though no longer that of Christianity but of a dissolved Christianity.

Bauer asks the Jews to break with the tradition of the Christian religion, a demand, which, as he himself admits, does not jibe with Jewish nature.

Since, toward the end of his study, Bauer views Judaism as a mere religious criticism of Christianity, it was to be expected that he would view Jewish emancipation as a philosophical and theological act.

Bauer takes the ideal, abstract nature of the Jew— that is, his religion—as his whole nature. He therefore correctly concludes: "The Jew contributes nothing to humanity when he disregards his limited Law, when he abolishes his Judaism."

The relation between Jews and Christians is therefore as follows: The Christian's only interest in Jewish emancipation is a general, humanitarian, theoretical one. Judaism is a fact offensive to the Christian's religious eye. As soon as his eye ceases to be religious, however, the fact ceases to offend him. And so Jewish emancipation in itself involves no work for the Christian.

But the Jew who wants to be emancipated has to do not only his own work but that of the Christian as well —such as the higher criticism of the Gospels, *The Life of Jesus, etc.*

"They may look on; they will determine their own fate; but history will not be mocked."

Let us break the theological framing of the question. For us the question of Jewish capacity for emancipation becomes the question of which element in society must be overcome in order to abolish Judaism. For the Jews capacity for emancipation depends on the

Jews' relation to the emancipation of our whole en-slaved world.

Let us look at the real Jew of our time; not the Jew of the Sabbath, whom Bauer considers, but the Jew of everyday life.

What is the Jew's foundation in our world? Material necessity, private advantage.

What is the object of the Jew's worship in this world? Usury. What is his worldly god? Money.

Very well then; emancipation from usury and money, that is, from practical, real Judaism, would constitute the emancipation of our time.

The organization of society so as to abolish the preconditions of usury, and hence its possibility, would render the Jew impossible. His religious conviction would dissolve like a stale miasma under the pressure of the real life of the community. On the other hand, should the Jew recognize his materialistic nature as valueless and work for its abolition, he would be working for simple human emancipation and the shedding of his development to date, thus rejecting the highest practical expression of human self-alienation.

Thus we recognize in Judaism generally an anti-social element which has reached its present strength through a historical development in which the Jews eagerly collaborated. Jewish emancipation means, ultimately, the emancipation of humanity from Judaism.

The Jew has already emancipated himself in the Jewish way: "The Jew, who is, for example, merely tolerated in Vienna, determines by his money power the fate of the entire German Empire. The Jew, who is without rights in the smallest German state, decides the fate of Europe. . . .

"While corporations and guilds are closed to the Jew or are not yet favorable to him, the daring of private industry mocks the obstinacy of medieval institutions." (*The Jewish Question.*)

This is no isolated fact. The Jew has emancipated himself in the Jewish fashion not only by acquiring money power but through money's having become (with him or without him) the world power and the Jewish spirit's having become the practical spirit of the Christian peoples. The Jews have emancipated themselves to the extent that Christians have become Jews.

"The pious and politically free inhabitant of New England," reports Colonel Hamilton, "is a kind of Laocoon who makes not the slightest effort to free himself from the snakes which are strangling him. Mammon is the God of these people: they worship him not only with their lips but with all the powers of their bodies and soul. The earth in their eyes is nothing but one great stock exchange and they are convinced that they have no other mission here below than to become richer than their neighbors. Usury has taken hold of all their thoughts, excitement derives from some change in its object. When they travel, they carry their office or store, so to speak, with them on their backs and speak of nothing but interest and profits and if they turn their eyes for an instant from their own business it is only to turn them to the business of others."

Indeed, the materialistic rule of the Jew over the Christian world has in the United States reached such everyday acceptability that the propagation of the Gospels, the teaching of Christianity itself, has become an article of commerce, and the bankrupt merchant deals in Gospels just as the enriched gospeler deals in business. *"Tel que vous le voyez à la tête d'une congrégation respectable a commencé par être marchand; son commerce étant tombé, il s'est fait ministre; cet autre a débuté par le sacerdoce, mais des qu'il a eu quelque somme d'argent à la disposition, il a laissé la chaire pour le négoce. Aux yeux d'un grand nombre, le ministère religieux est une véritable carrière industrielle."* ("The man who is now leading a respectable congregation may have started out as a merchant; his

-39-

business having failed, he became a minister. Another started out as a minister; but as soon as he accumulated some money, he left the pulpit and went into business. In the eyes of many people, religious ministry is a genuine business career.") (Beaumont, *op. cit.*)

Bauer holds that it is a fiction to state that the Jew is deprived of political rights while in practice he wields enormous power and exercises wholesale a political influence whose retail use is denied him.

The contradiction between this actual political power and Jews' political rights is the universal contradiction between politics and the power of money. Theoretically, the first stands over the second; in practice it has become its slave.

Judaism has maintained itself alongside Christianity not only as a religious criticism of Christianity, and as an official questioner as to its religious origin, but also because the materialistic spirit of Judaism has kept itself alive in Christian society and achieved there its highest expression. The Jew who remains a special member of bourgeois society is only a special phenomenon of Judaism within that society.

Judaism has maintained itself not in spite of, but because of, history.

Bourgeois society continuously brings forth the Jew from its own entrails.

What was the essential foundation of the Jewish religion? Practical needs, egotism.

The monotheism of the Jew is therefore actually a

polytheism of many needs, and it makes even renunciation the object of divine law. Practical need, egotism, is the underlying principle of bourgeois society and is recognizable as such immediately this society sets up its own political state. The god of practical needs and private interest is money.

Money is the zealous one God of Israel, beside which no other God may stand. Money degrades all the gods of mankind and turns them into commodities. Money is the universal and self-constituted value set upon all things. It has therefore robbed the whole world, of both nature and man, of its original value. Money is the essence of man's life and work, which have become alienated from him. This alien monster rules him and he worships it.

The God of the Jews has become secularized and is now a worldly God. The bill of exchange is the Jew's real God. His God is the illusory bill of exchange.

The view of nature gained under the dominion of money and private property is a genuine contempt, a materialistic degradation of nature, such as exist in Jewish religion, if only in fancy.

It is in this sense that Thomas Münzer complains that "all creatures have become property, the fish in the water, the birds in the air, the plants on the ground —the creatures, too, must become free."

What is stated as theory in Jewish religion, namely, contempt for theory, art, history and man as an end in himself, is an actual and conscious point of view, held to be virtuous by the man of money. Even the relations between the sexes, between man and woman, become an object of commerce. The woman is auctioned off.

The chimerical nationality of the Jew is the true nationality of the merchant, of the man of money.

The law of the Jew, lacking all solid foundation, is only a religious caricature of morality and of law in general, but it provides the formal rites in which the world of property clothes its transactions.

Jewish Jesuitism—that practical Jesuitism which in the Talmud, as Bauer shows, deals with the clever circumvention by the world of private interest of the laws that rule it—is the chief art of that world.

The transactions of this world within its own laws

are, indeed, necessarily a constant abrogation of real law.

The Jew obeys his laws not because they express his will and nature but because man is dominated by these laws and will be punished for transgressing them.

The religion of practical necessity can, by its very nature, achieve perfection only through practice, because practice is its truth.

Jewry cannot create a new world; it can only draw the world's new-made creations and relationships into the sphere of its industriousness, because practical need, whose motivation is private interest, acts passively and never initiates growth, only feeds on the growth of society.

Jewry reaches its peak with the perfection of bourgeois society; but bourgeois society reaches perfection only in the Christian world. Only under the rule of Christianity, which externalizes all human relationships —national, natural, ethical and theoretical—could bourgeois society isolate itself entirely from the life of the state, destroy all those bonds that link man as a species, replace them with egotism and the demands of private interest, and dissolve the human world into a world of atomized and mutually hostile individuals.

Christianity sprang from Judaism; it has now dissolved itself back into Judaism.

The Christian was from the start the theorizing Jew; the Jew therefore the practical Christian, and the practical Christian has once more become Jew.

Christianity overcame real Judaism in appearance only. It was too refined, too spiritual, to abolish raw material needs save by elevating them into the wild blue yonder.

Christianity is the sublime thought of Judaism, Judaism is the everyday practical application of Christianity. But this application could become universal only after Christianity had been theoretically perfected as the religion of self-alienation of man, from himself and from nature.

Only then could Jewry become universally dominant and turn alienated man and alienated nature into alienable, salable objects, subject to the serfdom of egotistical needs and to usury.

Sale is the practice of alienation. Just as man, so long as he is engrossed in religion, can objectify his nature only by turning it into an alien and fantastic being, so, when he is dominated by egotistical needs, can he busy himself in production only by putting his products in the power of an alien being and bestowing upon him his own alien products the value of money.

The Christian egotism of salvation is inevitably turned in practice into the materialistic egotism of the Jew, heavenly need into earthly, subjectivity into private interest. We explain the Jew's tenacity not by his religion but rather by the human foundation of his religion—practical need, egotism.

Since the real nature of the Jew is amply fulfilled in bourgeois society, this society could hardly convince the Jew that his religious nature (which is only the ideal form of practical necessity) is not real. And so we find the real nature of today's Jew not only in the Pentateuch and the Talmud but in contemporary society as well—not as a theoretical but as a highly empirical fact, and not only as a limitation upon the Jew but as a Jewish limitation upon society.

As soon as society can abolish the empirical nature of the Jew, that is, usury and its preconditions, being a Jew will become impossible because his conviction will no longer have any object, since the subjective basis of Judaism (practical necessity) will have become humanized and the conflict between man as a sensual individual and as a species will have been abolished.

The social emancipation of Jewry is the emancipation of society from Jewry.

FURTHER COMMENT ON
"THE JEWISH QUESTION"

Contrary to the masses the "intellectual" behaves critically by regarding his own narrow-minded work as absolute and its opponents as sinners. In his first reply to the critics of his work (*The Jewish Question*), Bauer reveals no awareness of its shortcomings but insists that he has traced the true and universal (*sic*) significance of the Jewish question. His further reply will force him to admit his "oversight."

"The reception of my work proves that those who have spoken for freedom and who still do so are precisely those who must rebel against the intellect. The defense of my work, to which I will now devote myself, will offer further proof of how lacking in thought are the spokesmen of the masses who think they achieve giant stature when they talk about emancipation and 'human rights.' "

The "masses" must evidently have begun to prove their opposition to the "intellectual" in connection with this work of absolute criticism, since their very existence is conditioned and proved by their opposition to absolute criticism.

The polemics of some liberal and rationalist Jews against Professor Bauer's *Jewish Question* have naturally quite different critical implications from the mass polemics of liberals against philosophy and of rationalists against Strauss. Incidentally, this quotation from Hegel shows just how original the phrase used above is: "The special form of bad conscience which manifests itself in the type of oratory to which that kind of [liberal] shallowness is prone, is noticeable, in the first place, in its talk of the intellect when it is least intellectual and in being most lifeless when it talks about life."

As regards "human rights" an article "On the Jewish Question," in the *Deutsch-Französische Jahrbücher*, proves that it is not the spokesman of the masses but Professor Bauer himself who has misunderstood their nature and abused them dogmatically. Compared with his objection that human rights are not "inborn"—a discovery made countless times in England forty years ago—Fourier's argument that fish, animals, and so on have natural rights is the argument of a genius.

We quote here only a few examples of Professor Bauer's contest with Philippson, Hirsch and Company. Even these feeble enemies are not conquered by absolute criticism. Professor Philippson is by no means talking nonsense, as the absolute critic believes, when he voices this objection: "Bauer is thinking out a peculiar kind of state . . . the philosophical ideal of a state." Professor Bauer, who confused the state with humanity, human rights with man, and political emancipation with human emancipation, had of necessity to invent a peculiar state, the philosophical ideal of a state, even if he did not think one out.

"Herr Hirsch, instead of writing down his elaborate sentence, should rather have refuted my argument that the Christian state, because a certain religion is its very principle of life, cannot grant . . . the adherents of another religion full equality."

If Hirsch had really refuted Professor Bauer's argument, and shown that the exclusively Christian state is not only an imperfect state but even an imperfect Christian state, Professor Bauer would have replied as he did previously: "Reproaches are irrelevant in this connection." To Professor Bauer's statement, "By pressing against the elastic spring of history the Jews have produced a counter pressure," Professor Philippson answers correctly: "Then they must have had some influence on history, and since it is Herr Bauer who says so he must be wrong when he says that they have contributed nothing to modern culture." Herr Bauer answers: "A thorn in the eye is also a contribution— but does it contribute to my eyesight?" But a thorn that has been in the eye since birth (like Judaism in the Christian world), growing and shaping itself with my eye, is not an ordinary thorn, but a miraculous thorn which belongs in my eye and which must have somehow contributed to the growth of my vision. The critical "thorn" does not prick Professor Hirsch. Besides, Professor Bauer's view of the importance of Judaism in "the formation of modern culture" has been well refuted in the work mentioned above.

The theological representative of absolute criticism felt so injured when a Rhineland deputy to the Landtag said that "the Jews are perverse in their own Jewish way, not in our so-called Christian way" that it later called him to task for using such an argument.

Professor Bauer comments on the statement of another deputy that "civic equality of Jews can exist only where there are no Jews," by saying: "Right. And right only when the other term of criticism, which I achieved in my work, is also present," namely that Christianity, too, must cease to exist.

In his first reply to the attacks on his *Jewish Question*, the absolute critic still insists that the abolition of religion and atheism are the necessary condition of bourgeois society. He thus reveals that he has not better insight into the nature of the state than that proved by the "oversight" of his work.

The absolute critic is vexed when something which he claims as the latest scientific knowledge is proved to be generally known. A deputy from the Rhineland remarks: "Nobody has stated that France and Belgium are distinguished by a particular clarity in the recognition of their principles." The absolute critic might answer that this statement was projecting the present into the past by claiming that the chronic inadequacy of French political principles today is a traditional state of affairs. But the absolute critic would gain little from such a reply. He must, instead, claim the obsolete view as the present view and the present view as a deep secret, yet to be revealed to the masses by his critical studies.

He must therefore say: "This idea (the antiquated prejudice) has been stated by many (the masses); but a thorough investigation of history will prove that, after France's accomplishment, there remains much to be done about the understanding of principles." And so even thorough historical investigation will achieve no understanding of principles, but merely prove that there is still much to be done on the subject. Quite an assumption, especially after the great works of Socialism!

Much is contributed toward an understanding of present-day social conditions by Professor Bauer's remark: "The present ruling certainty is uncertainty." When Hegel says that the present ruling Chinese certainty is "to be" and the Indian one "nothingness," etc., the absolute critic joins him in "pure" fashion when he reduces the character of our time to the category of "uncertainty," and all the more purely since "uncertainty" belongs, together with "to be" and "nothingness," in the first chapter of speculative logic, that of "quality."

We cannot take leave of the reader without making a general remark on the first contribution to *The Jewish Question.*

A main task of absolute criticism is to place all questions of the day in their appropriate form. It does not answer real questions, but substitutes others for them. It must first turn the questions of the day into "critical-critical" questions. If it is a matter of the Code Napoleon, it would first prove that it is a matter of the Pentateuch. It makes questions topical by critically twisting and distorting them. And so it twisted the Jewish question in such a way that the political emancipation with which it pretended to deal no longer needed to be investigated, and a criticism of Jewish religion and a description of the Christian-German state were made to act as substitutes.

This method, like all the methods of absolute criticism, is merely the repetition of a speculative joke. Speculative philosophy, that is, Hegel's philosophy, first had to translate all questions from the language of every sound common sense into the language of the speculating intellect and turn every real question into a speculative question before it could answer it. Once speculation had twisted my question in my mouth, and then, like the Catechism, put the question back into my mouth, it could, like the Catechism, have a ready answer for each of my questions.

CPSIA information can be obtained
at www.ICGtesting.com
Printed in the USA
BVHW082031300722
643443BV00001B/36

9 780806 529530